Whins

for Leslie

Whins

George Gunn

Chapman Publishing
1996

Published by
Chapman
4 Broughton Place
Edinburgh EH1 3RX
Scotland

The publisher acknowledges the financial assistance
of the Scottish Arts Council

A catalogue record for this volume is
available from the British Library.
ISBN 0-906772-72-9

Chapman New Writing Series
Editor Joy Hendry
ISSN 0953-5306

Some of the poems and versions of the poems have
appeared in or been broadcast on the following:

*Chapman, Northwords, Cencrastus, Northlight, Spectrum, West
Coast magazine, BBC Radio Scotland, The Scotsman, The Press &
Journal, Grampian TV*. Several of the poems appeared in the
"Whins Portfolio" limited edition from *Bonfire Editions*,
Edinburgh, 1994

Printed by
Mayfair Printers
Print House
William Street
Sunderland
Tyne and Wear

Contents

Part Four: Whins

Introduction

The bard George Gunn is a namesake, and by the same token, fellow clansman, of the distinguished Caithnessian novelist Neil M. Gunn. No-one reading George's poems, gathered here in this volume, can doubt that the geography and history of that redoubtable Pictish-Viking-Gaelic corner of the North Highlands have played as dominant a role in his developing political-psychological world-view as they did in Neil's well documented psycho-sensual pilgrimage. But whereas Neil's path seems in retrospect increasingly one of a rather misty otherworldly Celtic spirituality, George's is revealed here as representing quite another Celtic tradition – one of the gallus hard-headed satirical lyricism.

A perceptive analysis of Neil's journey back into "the lost land of hazel nuts and heather root" is found in Jan Curtis's essay 'The Celtic Tradition of the Winged Poet and the Mythical Salmon of Wisdom in Neil Gunn's *Highland River* published in *Scottish Literary Journal*, November 1995. Curtis writes: "Kenn's quest for wisdom in *Highland River* leads him across the pastel boundary between time and the timeless 'far country of legendary names' from which he returns, like the winged poet, to reveal the ancient wisdom of the folk". This is an admirable summary of Neil's metaphysical quest in this book, but it clearly will not do for George Gunn. Indeed, if one were to search for one single phrase which might encapsulate George's attitude to Scotland and Scottish history, one could hardly find a better one than George Buchanan's classic phrase *ingenium perfervidum Scotorum*.

This is not to say that George's poems are not as well and truly impregnated with the sights, smells and sounds of that delectable Caithness-Sutherland borderland as are the works of his famous namesake – and in some of these poems Strath Kildonan (alias Strath Ullie) has, for me, an almost physical presence, but the sardonic mental attitudes which give the poems their characteristic flavour remind one inescapably of other voices, in other places, and one finds oneself asking, who, and where, are this very gifted poet's "fellow countrymen of the mind?" . . . Reading poems like 'Shelley's Balls' and 'The Monument' (the statue on the top of Ben Braggie of the much hated Duke of Sutherland, duke of the Clearances) – not to mention 'Heiffer Hook' and 'Duck Egg Sex' – I think we have to look a long way beyond the braes of Strath Ullie. George Gunn's poetry brings together the quiet landscapes of the North and the loud political concerns of the contemporary world, and this makes him unique in his generation of Scottish writers. The force of his attack on his subjects disguises his technical control. The passion and inventiveness of his poetry recalls the great Pablo Nerudo.

Nearer home, across the Irish Sea, we can maybe discern the features of the late Monoghan-born Dublin city-dweller Patrick Kavanagh, who wrote *The Great Hunger, Come Dance with Kitty Stabling* and *Sensational Disclosures*:

> Kavanagh tells all,
> Lays bare his soul
> For the good of his neighbours
> And the Sunday papers,
> Patiently he labours
> To advise and warn
> Poets soft in the horn,
> Rising from his own dirt
> He sends this sensational report.

> He frittered away
> A talent that could flay
> D. J. Enright – say,
> He could disburse
> A fabularity of verse,
> Could swallow without dodgery
> Ted Hughes' menagerie;
> He often spat forth
> Lions of more wrath . . .

One could mention other Irish poets, but I'd like finally to enrol, as another of George's "compatriots of the mind and the heart" a living English poet Arnold Rattenbury, who was born in China, edited the left-wing review *Our Time* after World War Two and now lives in North Wales. Here's the opening of his poem 'The Making', dedicated to E P Thompson, author of *The Making of the English Working Class*:

> "Poor stockinger, Luddite cropper,
> 'obsolete' hand-loom weaver, 'Utopian'
> artisan" – the list don't stop
> because yours drew to its end, nor hope
> stop at your death, nor the "enormous
> condescension", posterity.

Like Kavanagh – and Thompson and Rattenbury – George Gunn is well-equipped to downface that "enormous condescension". I wish his poetry well, and I hope many other Scots makars will join him in 'The Boat Dance'.

Hamish Henderson

Part One: The Geometry Of Slate

Heron

You are grey in your flight
over the Ullie like the geometry
of slate you manage
effortlessly your ancient swing

The river, brown in its frothing laugh
hoots & slaps down to Helmsdale
great bird of my imagination
will we ever stop smelling

the smoke & how it too
poured down here that week
of the burnings, blown out to the sea
in an aristocratic choke & how a ship

was lost in it, blind in tragedy's fog
& how she waited until night
& was guided to the shore
by the glowing thatch forge

of five hundred fires, Heron
you will taste the fish again
here in this Autumn, by your
thin fields, your red iron roofed

cottages, snug like prisoners
in a photograph of an old war
& those other dwellings which did not
make it & whose rounded stones

lie in the useless jumble
time gave as its pattern
to the silenced tongue
Heron, the wind blows now

smoke of a different nature
Heron, the sea now has become
too alluring, she matches you
colour for colour, she is washing

the back & the face of this
resplendent little country
but she is raging, she is raging
& the years won't alter her voice

Heron, she will whisper to you
of her endless harvest
that knows no season
or springtime, she will give to you

the drum code of her percussive reason
she will sing to you, bird of Strath Ullie
great free one of the empty place
she will sing to you & meet your eye

so be calm now, my slate bird
for your wings are at their maximum
stretch & you pull the sky
behind you like a sheet

did your friend the gull not tell you
of the green song of the sea
of the white music of its chorus
did she tell you of the yellow

golden sand & the taste of the salt
waves kiss, oh heron
she must've done
because you take me to that other place

where the dream's result
is kept in the house of winter
did she not show to you
of how our suicide friend

the stone man, how he still
stands upon his plinth
did she not tell you
the perfect graph of oppression's placing

note it well as you fly
how his back is to this strath
& the many others like it
whose spirits animals graze

on dust & echoes & how
his face faces the sea
where countless Gaels went
to taste the sour whisky of a bad deal

& whose only promise was
that in the big sleep
they pay no rent
Heron, note it well

Kildonan

Leaving Helmsdale & the grey
mist of the North Sea
winding up Strath Ullie like an adder
the strath of rowan, the strath of juniper berry
hazel, birk & the green fern
as purple-sided as a lyric
strath of my best success
& the yellow dust furnaced
into the teeth of Crowner & Mormear alike
& the ceilidh mor in the wooden hall
gentle as my love's neck & shoulders
with your blue vein river song
Kildonan, my Ullie, you are as time's orchard
in the cut of Sutherland

Two Escapes

You will come to me one night
as I lie dying, I think
with my wet sheets & my muscles
taut like so much useless
statue marble & dreaming
of falling I will not fall
but groan & your form
because it will not be really you
will beckon to me & I shall
shrink through the wall
from fear & the guilt of sons

2

Seemingly Patrick Sellar sailed from Banff
across the Moray Firth to Helmsdale
often he would do it, from property
to property, but one day
he almost did not make it
& had to run for the shore at Portgower
his craft broken up by the swelling seas
pity then that the black creel
did not snare him, alas
the common song of Strath Ullie

On The Beach At Cracaig

The wind blows down from
Bheinn Dhorain & Bheinn Uarie
& out into the Moray Firth
for the luck that that would bring
& a rammie of grey seals
turn their bellies to it
in affection for the west
the sea claps the shore with its regular applause
& the sky hangs like a wet mattress
on the machair behind
the spring lambs are bleating
& the cormorants slice
the morning with a dive

The Blue Boat

The blue boat sits as plump as an eye
beside the dilapidated pier
from which some boys fish
There are no lobsters for the boat
or its owners to catch
only the vast sheer ocean
for it to mingle its blueness with
for it to bob & fathom the essential
moonbound sucking of the sea
Some scruffy crows on the beach
beside you, blue boat, peck & caw
at each other & a dead skate
& the boys land a velvet crab & a cudeen
& the finger of Portmahomack points east
Behind us, blue boat
the mountains are shrugging
their shoulders at the sky
& history puts on its boots
& takes the dynamite path
to Bheinn a' Bhraggie
ah, blue boat, you wink at me
the shape of melancholy

The Monument

On the summit of Bheinn a' Bhraggie
squat & vulgar like a beer tap
the phallic evidence of what's gone
wrong here in the land of the Caittaidh

is primed & waiting for take off
In the pub, to the clunk of pool balls
they dream a gentle revolution
of whisky & poetry, country

& western pours from the air
like treacle at a Christmas baking
& the English voices which own
the street light up our disgrace

& wonder out loud about their MOT's
& the rising of interest rates
& the tide goes in & out
& the years spin & the hill

stays exactly the same by changing
constantly its colour & meaning
In Kildonan a two headed dog
guards a lochful of sunken treasure

In eternity the roasting herring
dreams of Dunrobin
& the seagulls are not impressed
The monument is going home

Ravens
(Looking back from 1964)

As bairns half blind
we were taken to London twice
to be shown Tower Hill
Buckingham Palace, Victory
& many another tribal totem
which in their tongue
of adoption warned us
"No longer will your kind
take freshly stolen bulls
to Thurso to be traded
& no horses will take you back
home to the deep strath
when drink & ceilidh
overcome you"

The clipped wings of the ravens
flapped at us then
like the capacious heat
of history windmilling its way
through the uncut pages
of a dropped bible
not pure before or after
& if we took risks
they were sold like cattle
beneath the oaks
so all these things emerge
as Ireland twenties
into Scotland nineties
find a home

Coombs Kirk

A mouth out of a mouth of Dunnet Head
Coombs Kirk, a bonescape
under the cleaning whiteness
of the covering sand, a bell tower

of marram grass & its peel the wheep
of the oystercatcher & shochad
sounding across a parish of links
& seashore, set firm between Dwarick

Head & Murkle, a shifting place this
but no sudden covering & uncovering
as at Skarra Brae, no whale tooth
necklace brought mystery to this gathering ground

but a tractor-shovels steel snouted rooting
Abrach Mackay on-board, oblivious
to the plague burial site
he sells to cementer, brick maker, road builder

this parabole once & still now a seabed
the base & material for the rise
of trade, Europe grew from such
mergings as this, the dune barometer falls again

2

Not far from our door Donald Mackay
opened the Devils box &
out poured a lather of the fairy
folk eager for tasks & he at a loss

for once bid them join Caithness to Orkney
with heather ropes & then completing
this they had to count
the grains of sand on Dunnet Beach

& on so doing & as a product of their addiction
they buried themselves deep beneath
the dunes at Coombs Kirk
where Mackay's master held his sway

To sell a house like this is no strange
thing, yet behind the sandpile
of forms what other Devil's box
awaits the weird sisters of economic burial?

19

The First Resting Place

& the sea will know them
soon, like a grinning Viking
on Bal na Keil beach
in the Durness of my youth
where I used to swim
with chieftain's teeth
poking out of a sand dune
I must've danced on your skull
proud one with your beads & anyway
I'm not big enough to be a total Viking
I bet your name was Gunnr or Gunnson
you must've been on your way
to Ireland or Lewis
but Donald Mackay got you

& pulled you into Smoo Cave
& the boiling blackness
that simmers there
then he tossed your bones onto a sand pyre
time & the wind did the rest
was your home in Orkney
or even Norway?
Your sword in my hand
I could cry revenge
a peedie Valhalla on my lips
& the sea on my tail

Going Down To The Crossroads With Robert Johnson

(For Johnny MacLeod)

I had a dream, Lyle Lovett
was playing in the Drill Hall
in Castletown, we were going to it
we'd been in the St Clair, fill

as a negro's voice & happy
summertime it was, the blues
hung around the lampposts, the crappy
bits of the village came in ones & twos

this indeed was a dream, we met Robert Johnson
across from Abrach MacKays
he ignored everything & said "Son
play me the truth, I don't need no lies"

he pulled out a battered brown guitar
you pulled out your dented whistle
the itinerant Dounreay worker
caught a Highland bus & primed the missile

other workers forgot, the dual took place
the music of adders from your lips
MacLeod, the black & white race
wurlitzed in your hips

Lyle Lovett plays to an empty hall
St Donan plays a saxophone
his music talked of a rise & fall
here we are white negroes, there is Robert Johnson

across the street going down to the crossroads
I said "I was educated there
it was a rough school, god knows"
then I awoke to the silent air

Behind The Blackboard

The chalk squeaked year after year
as fields turned from frost
to potatoes to corn & the crows
cawked a liturgy of dead souls & arithmetic

as somewhere the dream of a meritocracy
grazed like an Aberdeen Angus
a Granny Grind-guts chewed its cud
marched the aisles & spat out "facts

about the Empire" & the dream world
of Canaan we on-loaded as religion
she told us everything was there
for us & Peedie Swanson winced inside

when it was slapped to us that Churchill
who was bad at sums still
became great, a misty look
crawled across her fish-head eyes

& opportunity like Johnny Onions
appeared briefly in the strange summer
biked & dangling to make us weep
far as we were from its swinging door

She Seamus

I look at you across a grey firth
a shingle bank where perhaps once
I saw you hammer in a stab
that was always the best ministry
your stocky frame held & no secrets
no frost on the ground you strode
your state no work of art
just the land & your rough hand
wiping the sweat from your face
at a crossroads between four parks
you would be waiting for yourself
to come up any track laden down
with the sound of your voice & echo
with my blood in you calling me home

Casting off the world of men you straddled
their fury & arrived at bull
Ion of the sea slate north
about the shrinking estate
of a failing majesty
a hunter after a set of ditches
she-Seamus by the croft wall
you would parade your taurine
pride at cattle shows & Highland games
each muscle rippling out its own applause
a beef champion on a short tether
you speak softly to your game
& dart your eyes to the horizon
of a lean tradition & snort your curse on it

Intercourse

The house stands empty now
its heart blown to the four winds
two in the summer of their yearning
& two in the black clutch
of death's camp by Thurso river
we shall cross it twice yet
before we all settle into the earth's narrative
yet I should take again the road north to the sea
to the only sea that is real to me
to where two passions meet
in a house where nature's fingers
found a green ever moving language
for her ocean & her love
where I shall take you when we are one

Bull's River

Going back, cool June, five years later
the house stands empty of furniture & fittings
a stone shell on the Atlantic's lip
I cruised the yellow corridors

& stood in the vacant rooms
a vagabond in my own familiarity
a tatty witness to what we have auctioned
a body's space under the carpet dust

after enough of a sordid time
I plugged the gaps behind my eyes
& left the vodka bottle I had found
on a window ledge beside a fading

photograph of some Gunns selling a cow
so I took myself off to the Peedie Sannie
& there, shaking under the chin
of Dwarick Head I wrote on the sand

in letters two foot high
"Helen Isabella Miller More
ten, ten, eighty six
why is it you are dead?"

2

On a marble mantelpiece
I found a bottle of your
tranquilisers, little white
dots that set you numb

under the thin midsummer sun
I pitched them far out into the bay
from a rock off which
you used to swim, come

time & draw your craggy parallels
I give you a woman
who swam far out
beyond the headland

3

You are on the hill of death
& this the styx
I stand upon
if you could dance here

we'd have a full barn stomper

I'll go now, to the quiet town of Thurso
bulls' river in its name
there I'll sing my nature song
one of herds & one of blood

The Curves

The curves come, how time passes
the tides of human hearts
in their burning purpose
but always shapely, how handsome

they are these curves, & they dance
in old halls, in forgotten places
some distance away, by a beach perhaps
or a kirk, or maybe a hotel, & even then

we cannot be sure, for who are they
these dancers, these human hearts
what purpose exactly do they carry
what sublime line fishing is this?

& a procession passes every summer
a linear subjection of rank
German cars in a cruel dream
curves, curves, the dead know them & are glad

my little country, you are a light
in Europe, you are old coins
in my grandmother's purse, the usual
stories of Wick on a wet afternoon, & in the streets

waxed from the wind like sheets
like drifter's sails, yes our purpose
is in this, a small matter certificated
thought out like a song, a story, an angel

I am in this, I come from this flat place
where ships leave & return to
where conversation gilds its landscape
to tongue & the hungry heart of culture

more Norse than Gael but Gael nonetheless
a proud silent culture, more of a slap
than a handshake, no sentences
where a word would do, I struggle out of this

from this, better for it, a lyric notion
my purpose their purpose, my time
their history & my future
a tangle of matter & seawreck

how they used to pull it up, oh the dead
they are singing now, they are dancing
you should see them, to recognise
them is to be them, the dead are singing

they come here, they die here, they live here
& time for them is a number & there are
many numbers many times, my family
is a chorus of whispers but they were strong

but broken now they still insist, they won't go
not they, tall, dark, a flame
in them to keep them right
to make sense out of the dark tunnel

Part Two: The Chootch's Dream

Storm

(For Hugh Loughlan)

I

The storm swirls in from nowhere
special – Iceland? the sixty foot
wave north? all we know is that
it swirls up Victoria Street
a y corkscrew in the neck
of a gust, it hisses through
the masts & riggings, humps
over the nousts & pierheads
sends the ferries bobbing out
to roll & wait in the Flow
keeps the planes on the ground
& like a swarm of aquatic midges
the water frees itself from itself
raging across the firth to sting the air

II

The stone fins of Stromness are wet tonight
a nor'westerly slaps us shut
but we don't mind, we're good
at huddling: the weather's great!
it's what this town was designed for
it comes alive like some tiny mammoth
dug out of an old snow
The folk seem to spark "wae da wedder"
Summer was a thin abstract glimmer
now they know where they are
& they talk & they project & they reminisce
"Du mind last year, boy, da same thing"
from equinox to equinox the old dance
"I wish sometimes dey could droon dey bliddy
            English sailors!"

III

It never got light today
oh aye, the sun got up somewhere
but not here, the first big wind
hit us yesterday, coming in
from the deep Atlantic like a bad mood
it roared over Shetland & blew it flat
it hit Orkney like a wet kick
what wasn't tied up is anchored out
what isn't flying is grounded
sometimes we've been like that
no weather forecast, no warning much
only the effects of a big pressure
but no more, we've advanced
into instinct's gentle predictions

Rain In Stromness

The rain tames the wind
a stilling symphony
of liquid punctuation
it floods over the little town
its language pours down
the wynds, the closes
in the narrow slate streets
stone salmon feed on ancient
headstones, voices echo
from sunken flotillas
where do the storm's roaring
lions feed now, where
now that the rain has come
is there room for the chootch's dream?

Stromness

The blue green sea & the green islands
are waiting in the midday
of their time, the paved
street shapes the town
& the air is full of prawn husk
& the fat smell of a morning's baking
feeds the rain-soaked fishing boats
as they harbour in their tang
By sea we came here once
younger then in our substance
fresher in our longings
than the tied & fast lieutenants
of other peoples beating geographies
we came here with our dream

II

The quiet bird sings
a barn owl in a green
hayfield, mouse
eager eyes a chronicle
of hunting, I longed
through this like a rainshower
as the pillars of light
held Hoy to the world
I thought of us there
stone collecting, walking
a bright duo in a flagstone bothan
I looked home & saw
the angels of circumstance
flying over Dunnet Head

Yesnaby

Beyond you America
behind you Stromness
far from me now
the tides changing on you
as I walk the crowded mile
of Byres Road, you curve
in my mind like a film
I would run over your top lip
through an equinoxial autumn
putting words in the mouths
of fishermen & crofters
you speak to me still
a language of salt & gull & wave
Hoy over my shoulders like an uncle

Part Three: The Red Guitar

The Thirst Of The Moon

The thirst of the moon
will be met by the mist
of its waning self
as she turns into
wolftime, a faoilteach
of gale & snow & night

The thirst of the moon
will die dry in the mist
of its waxing self
as she turns into
maytime, a céitein
of machair & flower & light

Full Moon Over The Forth

Who do we need to tell us
that the world has shifted
retired snooker commentators
or Norman Schwarzkopf?

My blighted senses are a division
of the less opportune, your
pasty nuclear face
a teddy lunar foghorn

with the gentle touch that
stone was not its meaning
yammering as you come on
in columns & in rows

I beseech you, stop! or
the moon will fall & then
the tiny fragments of our great
Atlantic plan will be seen as just

that: ideological porcelain on a
corrugated floor of commissions
& boards & non-elected trusts
where your grin is like a bowling alley

as the Forth turns to iron

The Coast Of Fife

Like lead you are chiselled up in slate
the water pours off your glacier edges
like hot molten steel
your beaches scrub themselves
in the close harbour of their haven
how time passes here like a greyhound race
or an old song lost & trapped
in the hold of a Burntisland boat
the Forth tastes you in a wet kiss
& on her top lip you linger
a salt & pepper moustache
shaved of passion & pit head
a Wemyss cravat dumped in a harbour
a swinging club searching for clout

Aberdeen, April 1991

No point in going to look for the sidewinders
they've gone, as if a wave
bellied its way along Point Law Quay
& flipped them all into the Burntisland of history

spring is young among the daffodils & granite
Union Street shuts herself against the sunset
& I lean against my memories
like a trawlerman into a new gale

still, never fear, all is wrong with the world
this town smiles her spring smile
before a backcloth of nuclear red
& blue night sky purple sunset falling

onto the Phillipinos on Market Street
who cannot be moved to notice this
they are busy, they are turning pavements
into snake hungry labyrinths of danger

I have nothing to offer them or the town
save some questions: why at the beginning
did you believe them, the sordid dogs
of the deal, the cut & the promise?

Two Buzzards Over Glenbuchat

Two buzzards glide
on the zephyrs above Glenbuchat
gently they swing & hover
in the blue deep sky
of this white hot day in September
they cut out their aerial ballet
in a soft floating
choreography of silence
their brown speckled markings
are an effortless coding
to their insularity & perfection
they hang like two lovers
suspended in their sheer
limitless possibilities

lost for a moment
then reappearing in a sweep
of mystery from behind
the high patient hill
& again they continue
their endless dance game
of curve & tag & distance
which sets itself out
in its natural poetry
of ritual & mutability
then, sadly, as suddenly
as they had appeared
they are sharply gone
leaving the sky

like a blue window
& the now bald brown hill
like a discarded table cloth
after a wedding

Macduff

An anchor, a cross, a kirk
a trio of images hauled from the sea
the boats like houses
and the houses like boats
boats in the streets
houses in the harbour
a kirk in the head
a cross in the boat
an anchor in the soul
and the Moray Firth a salt taste
on my lips as one by one the fleet
leaves tonight turning houses into boats
into distant lights consumed by blackness
with the grace of Mannon Mhic Lear they go out to the hunt

On The North Train

There is a Thurso lad whose favourite words are
fuck and cunt & his voice
stampedes up the corridor
like a herd of stirks
&, & two others outdo
each other with stories about this
& that macho doing dare
as if, as if nothing in the world
has ever happened before
he spoke, on their way home
from the rigs, from the oil field
& meanwhile Ross-shire flashes by
Sutherland, Caithness, a coast
of swearing & time on edge

Periscope

Kilbrannan Sound is a silent sheet
of blue glass, deep in its fissure
mackerel rummage on a bed of sand
a shoal of oily sea zebras
cystically hoovering between Arran
& the green pointing fingers of Kintyre
no friends to them the mass caw & cak
beneath the basalt lump of Doon Rock
& the water laps the shore slowly shutting
the sleepy eyelids of a school
of dozing seals bobbing as they are in their dreams
now Carradale is hidden under
the morning smoke of all this
likewise the liquorice thin eye of a periscope

Eigg

In Memoriam Hector Maclean

To regain what we have lost
to clear the bracken
four times a year
for four years
before it's clear
before we can feed
our people
& graze our cattle
on strathbed & island
from dereliction to desolation
post it high
over the rooftops
where the white birds
of expectation roost

St Cyrus

Sand the colour of Forfar
the North Sea hisses at me
all the way from Holland
On the horizon there is nothing
save for the odd purple explosion
here in Angus they call a dawn
September is oystercatcher red, how far
from the thistle am I from you tonight
Hugh MacDiarmid, the water lapping
like Plato's lip and the brown sand
of my temperance a grainy chew
slapped out here in a permanent lisp
all those questions, those questions
no mouth, no tongue can answer

II

The moon like a lemon slice
dips in between St Cyrus Kirk spire
& the sky, most of the harvest is in
some fields are ploughed, the red earth

shows its belly to the crows & sings
a long slow song of winter
In the public bar they listen to John Lennon
singing about how war is over

& they idly discuss the best way
to bayonet an Argentine, a boy's
home on leave from The Gordons
a war in the head is a war none the less

I listen and my Presbyterian stomach turns
to vomit, they know the number
of nails it took to knock up
Jeezus and no guilty tinker is to be seen

their cross leans burnt and drunk in a corner
like a broken ladder
a charred religion of tat habitat
& wind blown spam grass

ah, the moon is covered with smoke.

Montrose

The skies are like velvet sheep
so beautiful this town
they didn't hang your monicker
on it

blue & brown & green & yellow
take me to a more perfect ·
setting & I will
say Montrose

baa, MacDiarmid, we all have
a dichotomy in our heads
declaring a pedagogy
& turning it into a state tool

we take the child's language
& put it under the heel
Marlborough's army is still
at the border, just to make sure

For MacDiarmid 11-8-92

To be so far adrift as now
from our historic place
to walk an empty street
to see an empty face
to catch your frightened breath
when a cold wind passes
to walk the unploughed earth
of a land no land surpasses

There is an empty space in Europe
that is shaped like Scotland
a two headed golden eagle
we fail to understand
but to build the ship, the ship of love
to seek out the unsung song
& sing it to the stars above
to come to ourselves & belong

both MacDiarmid & Grieve walked
this unwalked road, & walked her long

Scottish Poets 1988

Our words are like bales of ether
evaporating in the harvest field
of a poem or intoxicating us
as drunk as sheiks before they do
in magazine essays on dead writers
or misquoted interviews or the crack in bars

What point to this boxed card game
like bullets rammed the wrong way
down the barrel of a gun we blow
our heads off as we come on strong
inhaling the bit parts in a bigger play
all claiming authorship to a ring of iron

     a bundle of wool

2

Free me of iron, free me of wool
free me of the god-building tricks
which tie me to the past
I ask this of you selfless self
so that I may not be alone
& bridge the river I feel on my tongue

Democratus was right & Plato wrong
chasing their tails which Descartes caught
& Pavlov wagged, but right & wrong
are wrong & right, what are they all
except lists, the autistic dorsal
on the critical shark, a sequence of havers & dreams

     a melted watch

Language

Like treacle it pours & sticks
hanging off half a lug
blowing a gaff & stubbing
its doup on the neb of a nyaff
usually English & rightly so
blurring & slurring & ha-ha-ing
its dung tongue boug empty
promise of heels & leather
& pox eyed geographies
mapping its symbols & boundaries
on the back of a population
turning the spit on a rattling
argument basting the many accents of lies
& where I walk my fond babble clear, clear

Gold

Gold, a tourmaline of light, the air ablaze
& the ground a clean nitrogen green
To come from the city, a crow filled sky
behind me, going north to the buzzard
& the sea eagles turning soar
the world opens like a flower
I taste the distance on my tongue
& relish its oaten flavour & its salt
foxgloxes, rhododendrons, the eye
of the common daisy all welcome the senses
in a nodding easy comfort
& the sun on their greeting
like love's ecstatic badge
& like the birk the blood rises
with the sap beneath the bark
& June's silver wine drinks
into the red earth
with the whispered promise of summer

Glory

The birk forest shimmers silver green
& across the hill beats the blood purple heather
the rock black river sings to the sea
"the summer, the summer, the summer"

the bug like sheep have been freed from their wool
& cars hiss along the snaking road
the distant mountains move forward still
& the sky is a changing mood

in the hotel bar the murderers hang up their guns
& the cowing beaters slump in their shed
the Range Rovers are parked like a halted cortege
from the land of the living dead

the foxgloxes sway in the gentle wind
the rowan berries wait for their bitter end

The Conversation Of The Mountains

Young I was & sleepier then
from bed one morning
a hard try I could not make
my father bellowing about the need

for rising & I arose then
& came down stairs
"Are ye glued til thon mattress
boy?" he asked, I shrugged & said

"Let me tell you about the conversation
of the mountains" "What's
'at? Ay conversation
oh ay mountains? Ye'll be tellin

us next ye'r a bloody poet!"
Breakfasting in the afternoon
my beans firmly on my toast
I replied "Yes, it's true & it goes like this"

& he listened surprisingly & I said
"Ben More Assynt raised her grey
eyebrow one morning & said
'It's good to be here' A thousand

upon a thousand years passed
& Suilven stirring her rump
agreed, saying 'Yes, it is good
to be here but we must never say it'

The universe expanded & Time caught
the magic bus & came back again
'Yes' agreed Ben More Assynt
'We must never say it, never'

& the lassoo of several centuries
tightened & loosened on the neck
of the world, 'Will you two stop
your squawking' growled craggy Stac Pollaidh

'Or I'm clearing out of here!'
"This," I concluded "is the conversation
of the Mountains" "I've never
heard sae muckle troc" replied my father

"an can ye no eat decent like?"
& went out to feed the hens
I yawned & turned on the radio
to hear someone lying about trains

Leviathan

Our land lies under chains
itchy bands around
the green possibility of Scotland
so we tried to build a dwelling place
but our doors have been forced open
the house has been
turned over & the furniture
lies askew & clothes likewise scattered
much money is missing
the occupants (that's us) have gone
there is no message or clue
as to where
The windows are broken
& the damage is great

On the roof of our house, our country
sits Leviathan
its head is rounded
& infected, its neck
is metallic & vast
its body a foul cave
where bad dreams find their manifest
it bellows of currency & power
its language is credit cards
& junk bonds
it excretes tourist brochures
& time-share chalets
From a distance it could be mistaken
for reason

Charlie Buckteeth On The Road To Damascus

One thing about Charlie, he would never have stopped
or been converted, his eyes too full
of the sky & the broad land
& if God was feeling that optimistic
then he could have no complaints
about the one-handed watch
he would be offered & at a fair price
but then God, being a bit of a Macphee
himself would admire the stunt
& Charlie would move onto somebody else
"God & the Macphees: all optimists"
is a saying of no known apostle
If I came upon this unlikely meeting
I know which one I would follow

The Basra Road To Ravenscraig

Sleet, the sky darkening
ever darkening
a face caked by flames
into a clay grin
eyes like a fish
stares into the back
of its own head
believing nothing anymore
because belief has blood
& skin & hair
& truth is blistered
metal & glass
& the day
the day is done

A long road
with a short turn
this the economic retreat
they fixed upon
but we are not looking
we're too busy running
running to nowhere
away from the storm
which is coming
our way with our names
on the inventory
of their purpose
our demise
their only plan

Sixty eight billion dollars
from south to north
fly like blackbirds
from a piece of sand
& forty third world countries
getting poorer because of the rise
in the price of oil
& in Lanark it's Wednesday
& the news leaks out
like waste from a sewer

onto Airbels Road
by the football stadium
sliding through the shopping mall
which will shortly close

The air turns to needles
& the eye
when it moves
catches cooling towers
& a grove of chimneys
puffing out a blue grey
green silvery cloud
slowly turning brown
as it drifts into the air
a sister to that other cloud
whose very blackness
turned the ground to tar
but now it's freezing
& the night is at hand

The eye winces but still scans
the tangle of buildings
& pipes linking
in a petrified dance
with conveyor lines
& tanks & smoke
signalling to us
a politics of design
on a dug up track
at the wrecked end
of a warfare injected with dope
now left twisted & strewn across
the detox reality of the raped horizon

Here veins pop from the pressure
of living through necessity
& death yet is not a series
of rows & corridors
so I come into this poem now
because I can no longer
stay abstract & without
& my collar turns
itself up in Motherwell
my lip sets itself

against the cursing cold
for there's no hurry now
no need for my imagination
to call this place down

Uddingston Bellshill
Wishaw Motherwell
the roll-call of the fucked about
but nature damn her pushes on
an orange sinking sun
the only furnace fire
left here to warm
the thin peel
on the lilting moon
& did they see the moon
that day the conscripts scarpered
noses to home
& their backs
to the F-111s
& Tornadoes

On the Basra road it is said
that human beings disappeared
not from intention
or Persian magic
but from high explosives
simply that same thing
they will turn on the 'Craig
when the time comes to wipe
away the physical reminder
yes it's Bert Nobel's favourite toy
yes his best invention
& I see him strumming
the red guitar
of the United States Air Force

Red

The red faced dead who are not dead
but are pending, rise up like hungry seals
after fish on the early spring evening
in the mouth of a sea loch, preparing
for this apocalypse & what is there to offer
a line of expectants duly filing past
the open fast food hatch of delirium history
or my mouth or their boot, a leather
of teeth & philosophy jambokked
into the corral of one's own country
or how better to put it as we chat up the reaper
how much blood can we spill into our veins
& how long can we sustain a civil war
in our imagination, stop them in the street
& ask them what they think as they dream
in a long dead Hebrew of fish suppers
& the fatal last drink & the colour is still red

The Luggagists

Here come the Luggagists
pulling their weight behind them
as they sweat & carry
the nudity of their imagination
in the boxes & the cases
from one still point to another
from side to side to nothing
upon a trolley upon a van
stacked square & neat
yet pulling & pulling
here they come these terrors
so that they trample balance
& shiver from that lack of sun
here they come & here they come

Edinburgh Bookshop

The Daleks which live in the cash-register
& the electronic cuckoo that squats
in the phone mingle with the teutonic choirboys
who are gargling on Handel in my ears
all defy me to be alone
so I follow myself around discreetly
looking for that book I wrote myself
but on not finding it I & I give up easily
unperturbed I try to recognise other authors
no MacLeod, MacLean nor Henderson here
only skinny spines & crammed empty pages
the offal residue of a slippery tribe
I see the exit sign beckoning near

Duck Egg Sex

Gender is like a fresh
duck egg in a frying pan
once you've cracked it
you have to take it off
the heat immediately
then return it slowly
never letting it stay still
& when everything
is finally firm
you take it out
& eat it

Shelley's Balls

I hear three voices on the radio who could
put out the fire in old England's gut
with such vowley stuff it would
take the shine of linoleum, they're in my nut

or around a table, earnest & miked up
to the Elysium circuits
of what-nots & thingamys their ears cup
to their headphones so that they can talk about the poets

& Shelley dead one hundred & seventy years
sodden on drowning he tried to drink
the Gulf of Spezia he saw as the tears
flowing from Castlereaghs corporate clink

he & Edward Williams, too young & innocent
the voices would have drowned him now
we are drowning all & all content
to do nothing but go under & allow

& afterwards the radio plays a dose of Mozart
to prove that they jolly well know
all about this thing called "art"
oh show me the way to go

home, Shelley, Partick Thistle are on wings of fire
jaguars of a people's hope
moving forward to a higher
league, can the west of Scotland working class male cope?

They & you & me & them
kicking stones on a deserted shore
watching for the storm's truncheon
to pass, timid all of us, to the core

for we could not be more dead than now
on Radio 3 on a Wednesday night
a set of voices giving jaw
about collective will & the individual right

are fighting amongst themselves, self-contained
the Protestants, think I
some men got stabbed, it rained
Shelley, tell them about the necessity of atheism, then fly

I speak back to the radio voice inside my head
I say "His song has not gone, it's on my lip
but we are dead, dead
& T.S. Eliot in a Rangers strip

& the Galway bishop's fucking minds instead!"
"We've got Shelley's balls!"
Paul Foot heard some Oxford bred
rowing oafs yell as they ran back to their halls

& the statue of beloved Percy Bysshe
a heap of naked stony chips
ah, majestic literature of the English
to be so treated just watch my lips

so falling asleep just like my nation
I switch those counties voices off
& like a dog pissing in the Clyde my education
won't bark or stop, I breathe in the west wind & laugh

Jan Masyrik Bites The Street Below

Political murder or political suicide
I come back to Jan Masyrik again
his teeth biting the hard hard street
that was Czechoslovakia 1948
dead in his pyjamas, his own shit
on the bathroom window pane
a bottle of sleeping pills untouched
by his troubled bed
& his speech to the Polish
embassy scattered on the floor
Jan Masyrik, a sad bourgeois clown
or a rare brave soul in a time
when a father's dream is no longer enough
& a consistency of opposition means wingless flight

The Russian Revolution, Take Two

Going to Dundee on a beautiful summer afternoon
in a long awaited August of heat

meal factories & trees blossom
like the pulsating flesh of horses

the clouds are chipping the sky
like the gloved jokes in a comedians

azure repertoire & my mind fixes
like a TV screen onto a man on a tank

& how he is everybody's new darling
but he's not mine: to me he is

a dangerous demagogue in an uncertain time
when fresh dictators are waiting to come on

like actors from the wings & I wish
that they did have wings that they could fly

over the rolling fertile plains of Angus
where the barley & wheat & oats

are queuing up to be the colour of honey
& it will be cut as will

all dictators in the black cropping
before the light of morning where ideas

are baked in the oven of need
I say, the harvest has begun

In Search Of The Invisible Sean O'Casey

We set off from Bewleys in Grafton Street
& heard all about Sheridan
who at twenty three had *The Rivals*
up on a London stage & his parents
to the north of his ear, of how Yeats
Synge, Swift & many others
went to school there, Quakers
were & still are generous people
we were told, but no Sean O'Casey

we were shown The Bailey & Danny Byrnes
& the little bronze pages
of chapter eight of Joyces' *Ulysses*
which walk their way around the streets
but not so lucky is Bloom's front door
number seven Eccles Street
stuck like a painting on a pub wall
& in St Stephen's Green statues to everybody
by Henry Moore, still no Sean O'Casey

like a helicopter donated to the poor
I stand beside the bronze unlikeness
of Mangan's imaginative remembrance
a bad landing in a strange place
pitying sad Tom Kettle strung up
on the barbed wire of nineteen sixteen
& beside the fountaining waters of Wolf Tone
a tramp washes his hair & humanises the henge
of some stone mind, where is Sean O'Casey?

I marvelled at Trinity College & the Book Of Kells
Burke did this & Goldsmith that
but hitch the plough & read the stars
was not among them, still
I sniffed the summer air & took
my thesis to McDades where Behan's
belly in black & white winks
at the foamy geometry of elbowed stout
the night wears on, I'm looking for Sean O'Casey

down by The Abbey they're murdering Brecht
someone is being dragged out of the Liffey
in the north of Dublin horses get sold
along with frying pans & cassettes
no literary walk ever winds its way
to that quarter of the town
yet this is Sean O'Casey's land
the place where he is not invisible
& the cock crows for me, for Juno & for O'Casey

Annus Horribilis
or The Queen Dreams Of A Revolution

The Queen's got piles
& tragic fog
the year's too long
& all her lot have gone bad

"The Range Rovers need new paint
& the dogs are getting old
& bad tempered
there is no possibility of a revolution

more's the pity." How close was she
to the Romanovs? Not very
a deranged German cousin
married one once & arranged soirees

where the conversation was lavish
& the deluded talked about
great poetry, big symphonies
& the semi-country between semen

& caviar "It wouldn't have mattered"
not that that's her sort of thing
"poets don't at least ache
one to abdicate although that Hughes fellow

makes one wonder" Ah, the melancholy
of it all, she really knew
no-one, it was almost perfect
the church is run by DJs

polo's out of fashion, the Scots
have gone off her & sing
of independence "It really is
too dreadful, it seems to rain more"

her mother thinks she is a tent
"Or at least that is what she
told that young pup from *the Express*
& it is so depressing the amount of Australians

one is asked to speak to, I mean
what can one really say
to an Australian, they are just
too republican, now a revolution, now

that would be something
at least one could
lapse with dignity
into the pigswill of history"

Part Four: Whins

Horse

A horse stands silently in a field
muscles twitching like a song
it's waiting for the summer
the days pass by like a festival calendar
the horse watches
waiting for the summer
we hide our dreams
in the deep pools where angels swim
& the horse waits for the summer
its eyes dark from Gaeldom
its body firm as a good decision
& the flies, they buzz for
things unknown to both horse & man
drinking sweat from a woman's eye, you

Three Lochs

You swam across as brave
as an otter, three lochs
or at least one, it was so hot
we toasted like two presbyterian
kebabs & all the lochs
meld into one, you in
the brown water a peat
trout of my chest's heaving
as strong as an argument
you made it from side to side
& climbed out tall & pink
& handsome claiming nothing
although I surrendered all
suddenly growing wiser under

the truce flag of the sun

Cul Mor

We rose up to meet the heavens
like the poems of Blake
a song on the summit
of this impressive croc
Cul Mor, dinosaur of rock
you held out your lime-
stone fin & took us on
pointing our heads to the Butt
of Lewis & to Skye, for we
were in great need of your
panorama, two sun-dipped
climbers rising in their own hope
a cloud mass of touch & longing
their wants the length of the Coigach

Heifer Hook

To pull you over Rannoch Moor
a joy I would gladly repeat
through blood & war if I had to
instead I gloried in the sweat
& heart beat of that long road
& the beauty of your body behind me
the kingfisher, the heron, the finch
their feathers were dulled beside your eyes
the deer, the cattle, the sheep
the owl swooping low through
the ancient pine of the Caledonian forest
shrank back in comparison to the pulse
of your heart's wanting, the gentle rain fell
in homage around your hair, we moved on

Drumochter Pass

Now that night is falling
& I pass over Drumochter
the silver of the evening
turns to black
& the hills hold up the sky
a smokey darkening
of Scotland's spine
the light matches your eyes
& I reach out to hold you
where the glenside & the thunder meet
& I can smell you
on my tongue, the taste
of your wanting
this landscape where I put my hand

Flying Over Glenbuchat

Down there my love is happy
where the brown hills
rise around the Don
where the pheasant & the grouse
ack ack at the deer
where she can find her silence
& her space to sing beneath the sun
down there, way below me
the great Buchan heart
of the northeast beats
& she – its blood & its pulse
its size & its glory
I would freefall to her
I would abandon these steel wings

Boatdance

My feet dance by themselves
in the poetry of boats
& I wish I were in Kildonan
where our feet were four reasons
to sweep the floor of the strath
a brown carpet of Autumn's welcome
to Winter & the cold sky above us
a brilliant pockmarked face
of eternity's favourite uncle
The Milky Way
    O what is love?
the ground asked me as I ignored it
but the sea peopled my heart
with your voices fleet
& I listened to them all inside my head
& my feet abdicated their positions
as the ministers of loneliness
escapees from the domain of half a dance
they became boats, their cargo is toes
& the map of the perfect step

Dockan

The colours of summer are thinning
Autumn has her crayons out
she is waiting for her time to come
The green fields aren't so green now
& the sheep are looking fat
all along the firths & straths
the landscape takes its signals down
the wind tastes for change & barley
& the moon is full & high
I think of you in this Northern hairst
but you are in that Celtic town
far from these pale skys
although I could imagine you
running through that crusty field

Orkney Equinox 1990

An Englishman's yacht blew up on the holm
a wooden scuttlefish on the seawrack's lip
the sea a weeping school of wrestling
tagging the ferry in the Flow for ten hours
a clutch of tourists in a greasy tub
summoning Mannon Mhic Lear with their stomachs
on shore, through the teeth of the gale, we grin
& the town is washed clean along its noust ends
& the islands lie green & flat
a gate to the seafield of the sulking Atlantic
where graze the wild eyed legions
whose only mission is the mustering of nature's rage
you fit in well here, my dark one
where the night sky cradles her cosmic children

June Rain

As dull as pencils the rain draws itself
from the sky & fills the paper
of the street with its wet fingers
hard it comes down, then gentle
& clammy, the air, then clear & soft
like a dolphin's dream or cotton sheets
the rain wraps the city up like a parcel
& delivers with liquid nonchalance
a vision of itself outside itself
blending the sharp corner geometries
with the mothered roundness of the sea
to give us back what we had forgotten
we miss the sun like we miss each other
something burning brightly behind the eye

Whins

To be so spikey & smell of coconut
so bizarre, you will not
let me touch you
like my love you are
an army before the war
upon the side of a hill, waiting
but I have no command for you
nothing inside me save
what you put there
a sea of yellow
in a darkening world

Moat Street

I can hear a baby crying
& the soft rubber sound
of a TV through the wall
the raised voice of a father, then silence
then more crying, more TV
a chair is pushed back with a scrape
the dull vibrations of footsteps across a floor
in the street outside a car door slams
& I think what will you make
of this wallpaper like old semolina
& these rickety tables & chairs?
A woman's high heels clampon up
the tenement stairs & it could be you
although you would be in less of a hurry

Moon

When the moon is full the dangerous one approaches
see her wild green eyes
spin through the orbit of her commotion
great tides crash surf hard
inside her & on the beach
of her temper wreckage is strewn
like the necklace of Kali
Dark moon child, you follow
your silver goddess & ruffle up
the harbour, the haven, the anchorage
you become the sea & sing
inside your head the storm sung
salt songs of all the women
who have wrestled with the world
men & their machines have stolen
from them, you surge to the land of earth & heather
like an argument between fire & air
you are as a moving island
on its hot tectonic journey